SHOCK ZONE™

VILLAINS

ASSASSINS, TRAITORS, AND SPIES

ELAINE LANDAU

Lerner Publications Company • Minneapolis

Copyright © 2013 by
Lerner Publishing Group, Inc.

All rights reserved. International
copyright secured. No part of this book
may be reproduced, stored in a retrieval
system, or transmitted in any form or by any
means—electronic, mechanical, photocopying,
recording, or otherwise—without the prior
written permission of Lerner Publishing Group,
Inc., except for the inclusion of brief quotations in an
acknowledged review.

Lerner Publications Company
A division of Lerner Publishing Group, Inc.
241 First Avenue North
Minneapolis, MN 55401 U.S.A.

Website address: www.lernerbooks.com

Library of Congress Cataloging-in-Publication Data

Landau, Elaine.
     Assassins, traitors, and spies / by Elaine Landau.
        p.   cm. — (ShockZone™—Villains)
     Includes index.
     ISBN 978-1-4677-0608-7 (lib. bdg. : alk. paper)
     1. Spies—Biography—Juvenile literature. 2. Traitors—Biography—Juvenile
literature. I. Title.
UB270.5.L34   2013
327.12092'2—dc23   2012013841

Manufactured in the United States of America
1 – CG – 12/31/12

TABLE OF CONTENTS

Assassins. Traitors. Spies. Everybody's heard about them. We've seen them on TV, in the movies, and even in comic books. These characters live secret, undercover, and often glamorous lives. James Bond is the classic example of this kind of character. He's the **handsome movie star spy** who always gets his man. He gets lots of beautiful women too. Bond is upstanding and true. He works only for the good of his country.

But are most real-life assassins, traitors, and spies like him? No way! These people come in all shapes and sizes. And more often than not, they don't have honorable intentions. In fact, this group of people makes up some of history's most notorious villains. The work they do is often brutal and ruthless.

Daniel Craig dons a classy suit to play James Bond in *Casino Royale*.

You'll probably never hear about some of the most skilled assassins, traitors, and spies. That's because they work behind the scenes. They don't want anyone to know what they're up to. For them, a job well done is a job no one knows they did.

Yet you can be sure of one thing about these mystery men and women: their lives are often on the line. Being a villain isn't easy. Still, many people choose this sort of life. Just who are they? Turn the page to find out!

Spies are always looking over their shoulder... literally, in the case of this spy!

BENEDICT ARNOLD

Who's the best-known traitor in U.S. history? Did you say Benedict Arnold? Most people would agree with you.

Yet Arnold started out as an OK guy. He was even a leader in the American Revolution (1775–1783). He helped defeat the British at Saratoga, New York. While fighting there, his leg was badly hurt. The injury caused him to limp for the rest of his life.

Despite his military success, Arnold wasn't happy. He felt he should have risen higher in rank. He believed that others were jealous of him. Arnold felt they had held him back.

As time passed, Arnold became bitter. By 1779 he was no longer loyal to the United States. He began secretly working with the British. At that point, he was in command of the U.S. fort at West Point, New York. But he planned to let the British take the fort when they attacked.

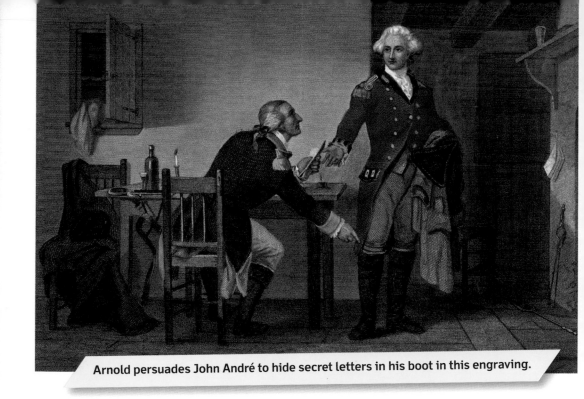

Arnold persuades John André to hide secret letters in his boot in this engraving.

Luckily, the plan failed. Arnold's British contact, Major John André, was captured. Arnold knew he'd soon be found out too. There were letters showing Arnold's role in the scheme. These were hidden in André's boot. André was hanged. But Arnold escaped to safety with the British.

From then on, Arnold fought for the British. He led British troops in invading Virginia. After the war, Arnold and his family moved to England. But he still didn't have the respect he longed for. The British never really trusted or accepted him. He died penniless and in debt in 1801.

TRUE OR FALSE?

There's a monument to Benedict Arnold's leg.

Believe it or not, the answer is true! It's at Saratoga National Historical Park in Stillwater, New York. Part of the monument is shaped like a large boot. It was built on the spot where Arnold's leg was wounded in battle.

BELLE BOYD

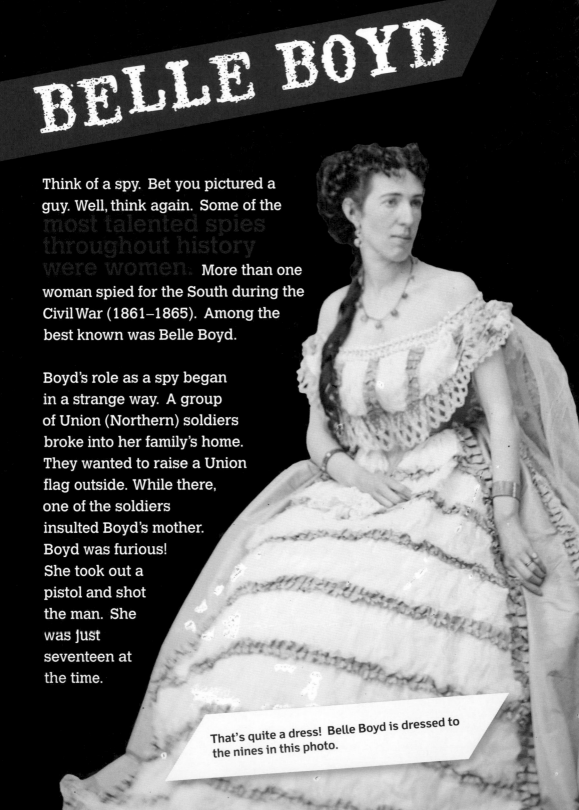

Think of a spy. Bet you pictured a guy. Well, think again. Some of the most talented spies throughout history were women. More than one woman spied for the South during the Civil War (1861–1865). Among the best known was Belle Boyd.

Boyd's role as a spy began in a strange way. A group of Union (Northern) soldiers broke into her family's home. They wanted to raise a Union flag outside. While there, one of the soldiers insulted Boyd's mother. Boyd was furious! She took out a pistol and shot the man. She was just seventeen at the time.

That's quite a dress! Belle Boyd is dressed to the nines in this photo.

Boyd didn't go to prison for the crime. Yet she wasn't completely free either. Instead, Boyd was kept under guard by Union soldiers. Before long, Boyd found a way to use her situation to help the South. The charming girl got close to some of her guards. At times, they told her what the Northern soldiers were up to. Boyd passed this info on to Southern generals.

After the war, Boyd toured the country. She spoke about what it was like to be a Civil War spy. Lots of people came out to hear this daring belle from the South. Her audiences seemed to find her every bit as charming as the Union soldiers had.

In gloves and a fancy hat, Boyd looks the part of a Southern lady.

JOHN WILKES BOOTH

In the 1860s, John Wilkes Booth was a stage actor from Maryland. He believed in two things: the Old South and slavery—which existed in the South until after the Civil War. Booth blamed President Abraham Lincoln for ending slavery. He didn't want Lincoln to help African Americans get the right to vote either, as Lincoln hoped to do.

How would Booth stop Lincoln? Booth, along with a handful of others, came up with an evil plan. They would kill the president.

They put their plot into action on April 14, 1865. Lincoln went to Ford's Theatre in Washington, D.C. Booth got into the president's theater box and shot Lincoln in the head.

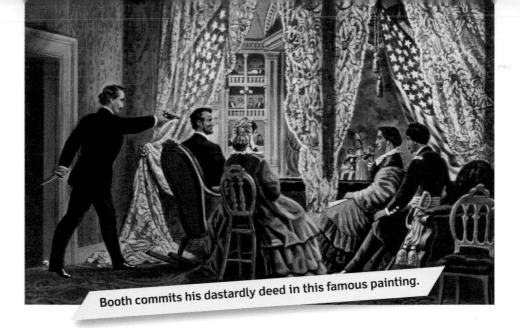
Booth commits his dastardly deed in this famous painting.

Seconds later, Booth jumped from the box to make his getaway. But he tripped and lost his balance. He fell to the stage below and broke a leg. Despite the pain, Booth limped to a horse left for him in the alley. He rode away.

Booth traveled to a farm in Virginia. Union soldiers went after him. They arrived there on April 26. They had come to bring Booth in. But something unexpected happened. Sergeant Boston Corbett shot Booth. He mistakenly thought Booth was about to shoot one of the other soldiers. Booth died hours later.

Four others who were in on the plot were tried and found guilty. They were hanged on July 7, 1865. Booth never became famous for his acting. Instead, he became one of the best-known assassins in history.

Boston Corbett, posing in a chair, was the soldier who killed Booth.

TOKYO ROSE

Her name was Iva Ikuko Toguri. But during World War II (1939–1945), she was known as Tokyo Rose. Some say she was a villainous traitor. Others say she was simply a victim of circumstance.

During World War II, Japan was a U.S. enemy. U.S. soldiers were sent to Japan to fight. American-born Toguri was in Japan when the United States entered the war. The Japanese government wouldn't let her go home. They asked her to go on a radio program that U.S. soldiers heard. The government told her to tell the soldiers that the United States didn't care about them. She was to urge them to stop fighting.

Toguri agreed to the plan. No one knows exactly why. Perhaps she feared the consequences if she refused.

When Toguri's program aired, the soldiers nicknamed her Tokyo Rose. They became very familiar with Rose's voice and message. So did the U.S. government.

When Japan lost the war, the U.S. government wanted to punish Rose. They tried her for treason, but she said she wasn't guilty. She claimed she'd only said things she thought the troops wouldn't believe.

treason = the crime of betraying your country

Yet Rose was found guilty. She was sentenced to ten years in prison. She got out early for good behavior. And in 1977, then-U.S. president Gerald Ford pardoned Rose. He believed she hadn't meant to help the enemy.

Still, some people disagreed. They felt she really was a traitor. It didn't matter to them if she'd said unbelievable things. They insisted that a loyal American would have refused.

Do you think Rose was a traitor? It's a hard call to make. Either way, she's remembered as one of history's most infamous figures.

Rose speaks to U.S. troops over the radio in 1945.

13

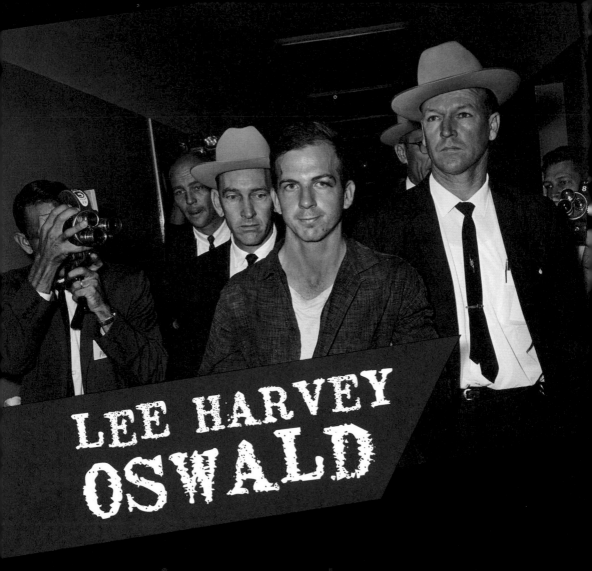

LEE HARVEY OSWALD

Who's the most famous assassin in U.S. history? Bet you said Lee Harvey Oswald. On November 22, 1963, Oswald shot and killed U.S. president John F. Kennedy.

At the time, the president was visiting Dallas, Texas. At about twelve thirty in the afternoon, his motorcade passed the Texas State School Book Depository, where Oswald worked. Oswald was there waiting for him with a sniper rifle. As the president's car passed by, three shots rang out from a sixth-floor window. The president was hit. He was taken to Parkland Memorial Hospital, but the doctors couldn't save him.

sniper rifle = a rifle used to hit targets from a long distance away

John F. Kennedy *(back seat, left)* and his wife, Jackie *(back seat, right)*, rode in a motorcade in Dallas right before Kennedy was shot.

Oswald hid the rifle behind several boxes of books. Then he made a getaway. He left the building just before the police sealed it off. But Oswald didn't avoid the police for long. Soon afterward, someone saw Oswald slip into a movie house without paying. The police came and took Oswald in. They soon realized that Oswald was the only employee who'd left the book depository earlier that day. They thought he was probably the shooter.

Oswald didn't live long enough to have a trial. Dallas nightclub owner Jack Ruby shot him as the police were taking him to jail.

This photo shows a reenactment of the famous Kennedy assassination.

Some say Oswald could not have acted alone. They don't think he was smart enough to pull it off. It's also been argued that he wasn't a good enough shot. Could Oswald have been part of a more complex plot? The question is still often debated.

WANTED FBI

CIVIL RIGHTS - CONSPIRACY
INTERSTATE FLIGHT - ROBBERY
JAMES EARL RAY

FBI No. 405,942 G

...ph taken 1968
...drawn by artist)
...James O'Conner, Jame...

JAMES EARL RAY

James Earl Ray was a criminal for much of his life. But on April 4, 1968, he committed a crime that shook the nation. He killed U.S. civil rights leader Dr. Martin Luther King Jr. Ray was a racist. He didn't think African Americans should have the same rights as whites, such as the right to attend public schools or the right to vote in elections. In early April 1968, King was in Memphis, Tennessee. Ray rented a room directly across from the motel where King was staying. Ray came prepared to kill King. He brought a rifle and binoculars. Ray waited until King stepped out on the motel balcony. At that point, he shot him.

On the day before he was killed, King (center) stands near the spot where the shooting took place.

Minutes later, Ray fled the scene. Ray's fingerprints were later found on both the rifle and the binoculars. As it turned out, Ray escaped to England. However, two months later, he was arrested at a London airport. The British were after him for robbing a bank there.

The British government returned Ray to the United States. He pleaded guilty to killing King. It was the only way to avoid a trial and a possible death sentence. He was sentenced to ninety-nine years in prison. But that wasn't quite the end of the story. Three days later, Ray changed his mind about being guilty. He said he was innocent and wanted a trial. But his case was never reopened. Ray died in prison on April 2, 1998.

Shocked friends and admirers of Dr. King point out where the fatal shots came from shortly after the civil rights leader was killed.

CHRISTOPHER BOYCE

As a child, Christopher Boyce seemed nearly perfect. He was intelligent, loved birds, and was an alter boy at church. Boyce's dad was a former FBI agent. His mom was a devoted mother to Boyce and a devout Catholic who'd once even thought about becoming a nun.

Who'd imagine that Boyce would one day spy for the Soviet Union? But that's exactly what happened. The trouble started when Boyce went to work for a company that did defense work for the U.S. government. Boyce got security clearances to do his job. These allowed him to learn about important government operations.

security clearances = rights to know about secret government information and projects

As it turned out, Boyce didn't like what he saw. He felt that U.S. leaders often abused their power. He rebelled against the system. In the 1970s, he decided to sell U.S. secrets to the Soviet Union.

Boyce asked his childhood friend Andrew Daulton Lee to help him. Lee had become a drug dealer. Boyce knew Lee would be interested in working with the Soviets for money. The two decided that Lee would approach the Soviet Union at its embassy, a place where many representatives of the Soviet Union gathered, down in Mexico City, Mexico. Their plan worked. The pair sold all kinds of secrets.

Their success didn't last, however. While Lee was on one of his trips to Mexico, the Mexican police accused him of another, unrelated crime. After days of questioning, Lee broke down. He told them that he and Boyce had sold secrets to the Soviet Union.

Boyce was sentenced to a long stint in prison. He didn't get out until he was fifty. The young man who'd turned spy ended up spending much of his adult life behind bars.

This is a scene from *The Falcon and the Snowman*, a 1985 movie about Christopher Boyce.

JOHN ANTHONY WALKER JR.

A federal marshal walks alongside Walker *(left)* after Walker was charged with spying.

It happened on the night of May 19, 1985. John Anthony Walker Jr., a former naval officer, was driving along a deserted road. When he reached a tree with a "no hunting" sign on it, Walker stopped his van. He placed a trash bag next to the tree and took off. The trash bag contained 129 stolen navy documents.

Meanwhile, a Soviet agent in a nearby area dropped off a bag for Walker.

Inside it was $200,000 in fifty- and hundred-dollar bills. The two men never saw each other. But that's how it was usually done. John Anthony Walker Jr. had been selling valuable naval secrets to the Soviets this way since 1967.

As it turned out, Walker didn't get his money that night. The Soviets didn't get their bag of secrets either. The FBI had learned what Walker was doing. He was arrested instead.

How did Walker get all the navy documents? In addition to being a former navy man himself, Walker had many navy contacts. He oversaw a ring of spies with close connections to the navy. One spy in the ring was Walker's son Michael, a seaman on a nuclear aircraft carrier. Another was Walker's friend Jerry Alfred Whitworth, also a navy insider. Walker's older brother, a navy veteran, was part of the ring too.

The Soviets learned a lot from Walker. They found out where U.S. nuclear submarines were stationed. They also learned about the secret underwater microphones the United States used to track Soviet nuclear subs. Valuable naval documents were decoded for the Soviets as well.

Walker had done it all for money. But he didn't get to enjoy his fortune. He was sentenced to life in prison.

ALDRICH HAZEN AMES

Aldrich Hazen Ames looked like a loyal American. He'd worked for the CIA (Central Intelligence Agency) for thirty-one years. But looks can fool you. He was really a traitor and a spy for the Soviet and Russian governments.

Ames gave the Soviets and the Russians the names of double agents. These were Soviet and Russian spies who'd begun secretly working for the United States. The U.S. government had spent a lot of time bringing the double agents over to their side. But soon many of these men were being arrested and executed by the Soviets and the Russians. At first the CIA didn't know what was happening. It later learned that at least ten of these deaths were due to information that Ames had leaked.

Ames paid in cash for this half-million-dollar house.

Ever heard the saying "crime doesn't pay"? At first, that saying didn't seem to apply to Ames. The Soviets and the Russians paid well. Ames made less than $70,000 a year at his CIA job. Yet he was bringing $540,000 home with the cash he got from the Soviets and the Russians. He bought a new Jaguar to drive around in. His wife wore fancy fur coats and beautiful jewelry.

But the cash stopped flowing once Ames was discovered. Both Ames and his wife—who knew about Ames's spying—were arrested. The couple pleaded guilty to spying activities in 1994. Ames's wife was sentenced to sixty-three months in prison. Ames got a life sentence without the possibility of parole. Crime didn't pay for Ames after all!

THE WIFE'S LIFE

At first, Ames's wife *(right)* claimed that she didn't know her husband was a spy. But the FBI knew better. They'd heard her voice on several recorded phone calls. She'd been giving her husband tips on how to handle the different people and situations he encountered as he passed information on to the Soviets and the Russians.

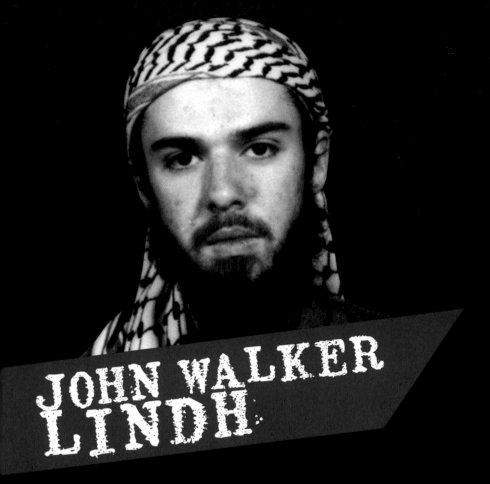

JOHN WALKER LINDH

The press called him the American Taliban. He called himself a holy warrior. Most Americans called him a traitor. But who is he really? The young man's name is John Walker Lindh. He's an American who'd left his country in the 1990s. By 2001 he was fighting for the Taliban against the United States in Afghanistan.

Taliban = a group of Islamic warriors in Afghanistan

Lindh, along with other Taliban fighters, was captured by the United States. He was taken to Qala-i-Jangi fortress. No one there knew he was American. He spoke in Arabic, which he'd studied enough to speak fluently. He'd grown a beard, and he dressed like every other Taliban fighter.

But in late November 2001, there was a riot at Qala-i-Jangi. The U.S. military put a stop to it. Many were killed in the uprising. Lindh was one of only about eighty men who survived. American troops found him bloodied and dirty. When they began to question him, they were shocked to discover that they were talking to another American.

Lindh had become interested in Islam as a teen. He went to Yemen to learn more about it. He came back to the states for a while, but he felt restless. So he returned to Yemen. Before long, Lindh ended up in Pakistan, where he received military training. He joined the terrorist group al-Qaeda and was sent to Afghanistan to fight for Islam.

Lindh was brought back to the United States to stand trial. Many who knew him were shocked. His teachers described him as a quiet boy and a good student. His friends said he liked hip-hop music and shooting hoops. He seemed like an all-American kid. Yet this same young man chose to betray his country. He was sentenced to twenty years in prison.

John Walker Lindh is led away after being captured in Afghanistan.

ANNA CHAPMAN

Anna Chapman had always been bright. She earned a master's degree in economics. She started a successful real estate business. She had good looks going for her too. Everywhere she went, people noticed her stunning red hair, lovely complexion, and fit figure.

Does Chapman sound like an all-American success story? Well, guess again! Chapman was an undercover agent for the Russians and had been born in the Soviet Union. She was part of a spy ring in the United States.

Chapman's spy ring had done their job well. They had gotten close to high-level people in U.S. foreign policy circles. The spy ring's goal was to find useful information and send it back to Russia.

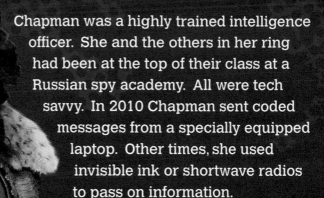

Chapman was a highly trained intelligence officer. She and the others in her ring had been at the top of their class at a Russian spy academy. All were tech savvy. In 2010 Chapman sent coded messages from a specially equipped laptop. Other times, she used invisible ink or shortwave radios to pass on information.

But Chapman's success as a spy didn't last. The FBI broke the coded messages she sent and uncovered the spy ring. Most of the spies in the ring were charged in U.S. courts. As part of a prisoner exchange program, they were sent back to Russia. In return, Russia sent the United States some captured U.S. spies.

These days, Chapman has given up spying. In a surprising twist, she went into entertainment! She works as a TV actress and model in Moscow.

Spy-turned-model Anna Chapman takes to the runway during Fashion Week in Moscow.

A GHOSTLY SPY RING

The FBI called Anna Chapman's spy ring Ghost Stories. That's because many of the spies in the ring took on the names and life stories of dead Americans. They'd mention these Americans' names and life details to anyone who asked them for their personal information.

ROBERT HANSSEN

How could Robert Hanssen be a spy? He just didn't seem the type. Young Robert was a quiet boy who went to church on Sundays. His father was a Chicago police officer. As an adult, Hanssen married a sweet, polite woman named Bonnie and had six children. Hanssen even followed in his father's footsteps and went into law enforcement. He became an FBI agent.

It was while working for the FBI that Hanssen got into trouble. His job was to protect his country. But he ended up doing something very different. Hanssen became a spy for the Soviets and the Russians. He provided them with important information from 1979 to 2001. At times, Hanssen tipped them off to the identities of double agents. He also gave away valuable details on U.S. operations. He supplied the Soviets and the Russians with information gathered through radar and spy satellites as well.

Hanssen put his country at risk. But why did he do it? What made an FBI agent turn on the nation he'd sworn to serve? It seemed to be the same reason why others had betrayed their country at around this time: they did it for the money.

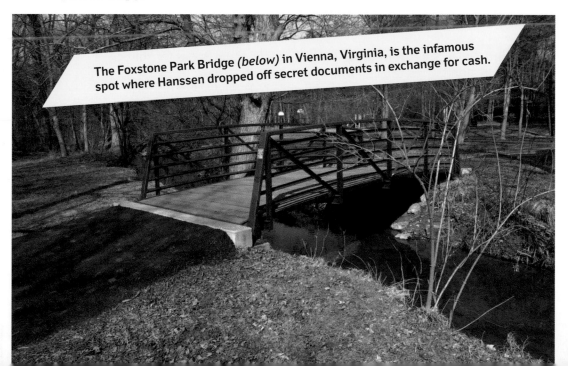

FBI video equipment captured this grainy image of agents arresting Hanssen near his Virginia home.

And the money was good. When Hanssen was paid in cash, it was often in one-hundred-dollar bills. These were wrapped in neat bundles and left at a local park for him. It's believed that over the years, Hanssen was paid more than a million dollars in cash and diamonds.

At his trial, Hanssen said he was sorry for what he had done. But it was too late. He was sentenced to life in prison without parole. It wasn't the future he'd dreamed of, but it's the one you often get when you're a spy!

The Foxstone Park Bridge *(below)* in Vienna, Virginia, is the infamous spot where Hanssen dropped off secret documents in exchange for cash.

Beck, Esther. *Cool Spy Supplies: Fun Top Secret Science Projects.* Edina, MN: Abdo, 2008. Make your next science project really interesting and fun. Choose a cool science experiment from this book and feel like a real spy!

Denega, Danielle. *The Cold War Pigeon Patrols and Other Animal Spies.* New York: Franklin Watts, 2008. Did you know that not all spies walk on two legs? Some of history's most successful sleuths flew, barked, and swam. Check out this book to learn about these animal spies in the military, on police teams, and even in the CIA.

Earnest, Peter, and Suzanne Harper. *The Real Spy's Guide to Becoming a Spy.* New York: Abrams Books for Young Readers, 2009. Here's the official handbook for kids who dream of one day becoming a spy. This interesting, fact-filled book lets you know what spies really do and the kind of training involved.

Farman, John. *The Short and Bloody History of Spies.* Minneapolis: Millbrook Press, 2003. Take a highly detailed peek into the sneaky world of spies.

FBI: Kids Investigate
http://www.fbi.gov/fun-games/kids/kids-investigate
Go to this website to see how the FBI investigates. Don't miss the link on spies. You'll find spy tricks, spy words, and much more!

Fridell, Ron. *Spy Technology.* Minneapolis: Lerner Publications Company, 2007. Read about all kinds of cool technology linked to spying.

Gifford, Clive. *Spies Revealed.* New York: Atheneum Books for Young Readers, 2008. This text is a who's who of spying. You'll learn the difference between a spymaster and a mole plus read about disguise masters. There's also some great info on secret codes and special spy equipment.

Harriet Tubman: Civil War Spy
http://kids.nationalgeographic.com/kids/stories/peopleplaces/harriettubman
Harriet Tubman is famous for her work on the Underground Railroad, through which she led many slaves to freedom. But did you know that she was also a spy for the Union during the Civil War? Learn all about it at this interesting website.

King, Bart. *The Big Book of Spy Stuff.* Layton, UT: Gibbs Smith, 2010. From secret messages to gadgets, this entertaining book will let you pull away the cloak of mystery from history's sneakiest sneaks—spies!

Platt, Richard. *Spy.* New York: DK Publications, 2009. You'll discover the often-amazing work of spies in this book. It examines spy activity from early times to today.

Schwartz, Heather E. *Gangsters, Bootleggers, and Bandits.* Minneapolis: Lerner Publications Company, 2013. Do you like reading about bad guys and gals? Then you'll love this look at some of history's most notorious gangsters, bootleggers, and bandits.

INDEX

PHOTO ACKNOWLEDGMENTS

The images in this book are used with the permission of: © Sony Pictures/Courtesy Everett Collection, p. 4; © Michael Blann/Digital Vision/Getty Images, p. 5; The Granger Collection, New York, pp. 6, 7 (top); © Wikimedia Foundation, Inc., p. 7 (bottom); Library of Congress, pp. 8 (LC-DIG-cwpbh-01988), 9 (top, LC-DIG-ppmsca-19388), 15 (top, LC-USZ62-134844); © Peter Newark Military Pictures/The Bridgeman Art Library, p. 9 (bottom); National Archives, pp. 10, 13; © Bettmann/CORBIS, pp. 11 (top), 16 (top), 18; © Alexander Gardner/George Eastman House/Getty Images, p. 11 (bottom); © Mug Shot/Alamy, p. 12; © Tom Dillard/Dallas Morning News/CORBIS, p. 14; © CORBIS, p. 15 (bottom); AP Photo, pp. 16 (bottom), 24; © Joseph Louw/Time & Life Pictures/Getty Images, p. 17; © Orion/Courtesy Everett Collection, p. 19; © iStockphoto.com/Susan Ridley, p. 20 (top); AP Photo/Bob Daugherty, p. 20 (bottom); © Mark Meyer/Time & Life Pictures/Getty Images, p. 21; © Jeffrey Markowitz/Sygma/CORBIS, p. 22; © Terry Ashe/ Time & Life Pictures/Getty Images, p. 23 (top); AP Photo/Dennis Cook, p. 23 (bottom); REUTERS, p. 25; © Natalia Kolesnikova/AFP/Getty Images, p. 26; AP Photo/Luba Sheme, p. 27; © FBI/Newsmakers/Getty Images, p. 28; © CNN/Getty Images, p. 29 (top); © Greg Mathieson/Time & Life Pictures/Getty Images, p. 29 (bottom).

Front cover: © Archive Photos/Getty Images.

Main body text set in Calvert MT Std Regular 11/16.
Typeface provided by Monotype Typography.